BIG BOOK OF MAZES

Kim Blundell and Jenny Tyler

Contents

Island adventure

Cat's rich cousin Lionel has invited Cat and Mouse to a party on his new island.

"He's sent two train tickets to Felixham, wherever that is," says Cat.

"And a complicated map," says Mouse. "I do wish Lionel would stop buying these cheap islands that are so difficult to find."

"Mmm. He does have good parties, though," says Cat.

Cat looked at the map. "It's easy," he says. "The dotted lines are paths and the wiggly lines are ferry routes. We can rent a boat, too, and take it where we like. Come on."

He dashes off to sort out his party clothes and find a present for Lionel. Mouse is still looking at the map, frowning. "What's Lionel's island called?" he shouts.

"They're always named after him," shouts back Cat.

Can you help Cat and Mouse find their way to Lionel's island? Help them find the island and Felixham station first.

Dear Cat and Mouse

Please come to a summer party on my new island on Friday. Here's a map. Don't forget to mention my name when you see Nelson at Renta Boat.

From your cousin,
Lionel B. Cross

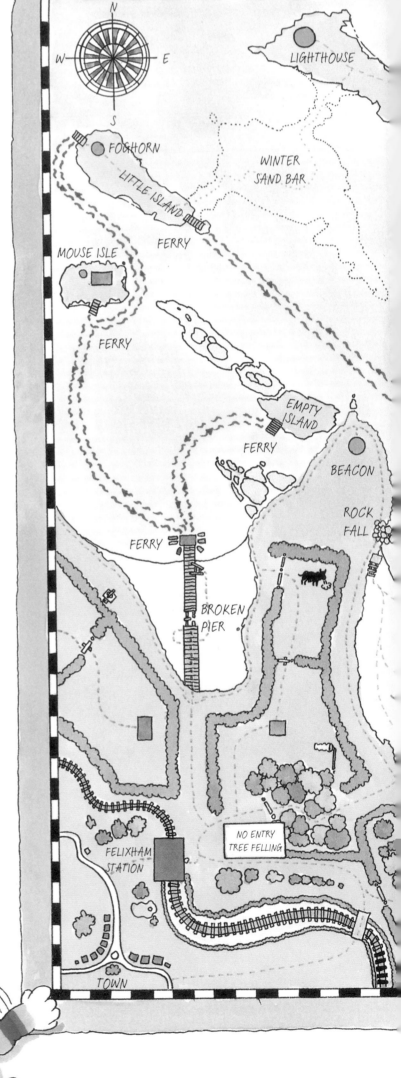

2

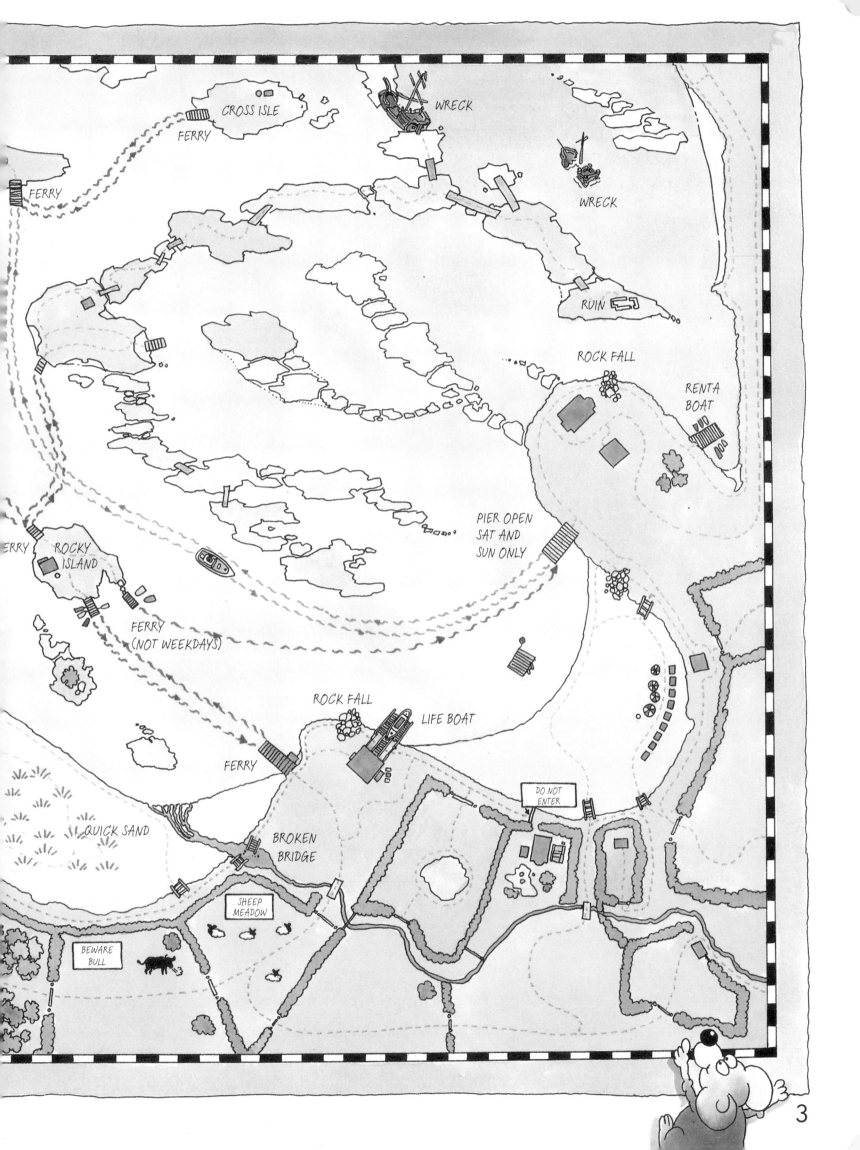

CROSS ISLE

FERRY

FERRY

WRECK

WRECK

RUIN

FERRY

ROCKY ISLAND

FERRY (NOT WEEKDAYS)

ROCK FALL

RENTA BOAT

PIER OPEN SAT AND SUN ONLY

ROCK FALL

LIFE BOAT

DO NOT ENTER

FERRY

QUICK SAND

BROKEN BRIDGE

SHEEP MEADOW

BEWARE BULL

Avoiding the animals

When Cat and Mouse arrive at Cross Isle, they find a note stuck to the pier, which says, "Party at lighthouse." They set off along the hedge-lined paths, but soon realize that there are lots of animals hiding in corners, getting ready for the party. They decide to choose their route very carefully so they don't walk past the entrances to their hiding places. Can you help them decide which way to go?

Welcome to Cross Isle

Party at lighthouse

Lionel is waiting for them at the lighthouse with his bodyguard, Vera Viper, and a sad-looking penguin called Pinkie. Pinkie seems worried that all the other animals are in pairs, and he is alone. (It is difficult to understand, as he speaks Penguinese.)

Cat says, "Don't worry, Pinkie. Wait here. We'll find a friend for you. Um, which way is it to Penguinland?"

"Try asking Surf Crab," says Lionel.

Before you follow Cat and Mouse, can you spot all the animal pairs?

Rock climb

Cat and Mouse follow the swampy smell and the signs for Surf Crab's hut. At last, they see it. Cat rushes eagerly and falls straight into the swamp. Mouse helps him out.

They see they must pick their way carefully across the wobbly rocks and rickety bridges. They need you to help them find the way.

Unknown to Cat and Mouse (and to each other), both Pinkie and sinister Vera Viper have decided to follow them.

See if you can spot them hiding in all the pictures from now on.

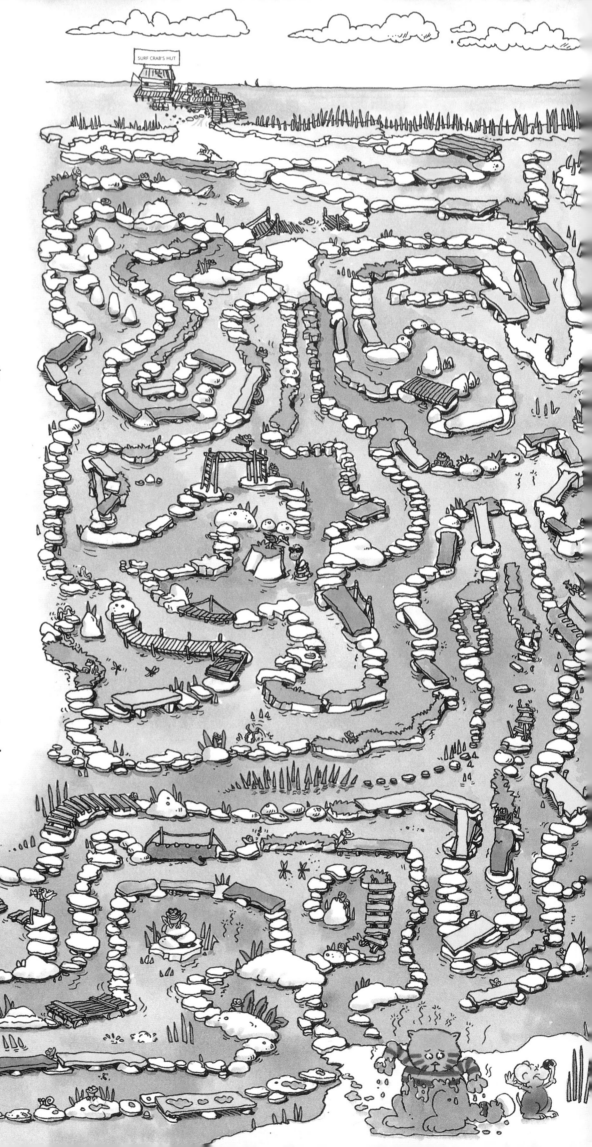

SURF CRAB'S HUT

Risking the rickety pier

Surf Crab's hut is perched at the end of an old pier. Cat and Mouse can see Crab's fishing rod so he must be there, but he doesn't seem to hear their shouts. They reluctantly decide that if they want an answer to their question, they will have to climb along the rotten and unsafe wood of the pier.

Can you help them find the way? They can walk across rocks and boats if they need to, but they can't untie the boats.

SURF CRAB'S HUT

Stick to the striped seaweed

Surf Crab doesn't know where Penguinland is, but he suggests Cat and Mouse ask Queen Conger. He lends them some diving equipment so they can go and see her.
 She won't speak to them unless they take her some red coral berries that grow on yellow and green striped seaweed. Blue and yellow berries give her a tummyache. Crab says if they follow a piece of yellow and green striped seaweed that has only red berries growing on it, this should lead to Queen Conger's cave. Can you help them?

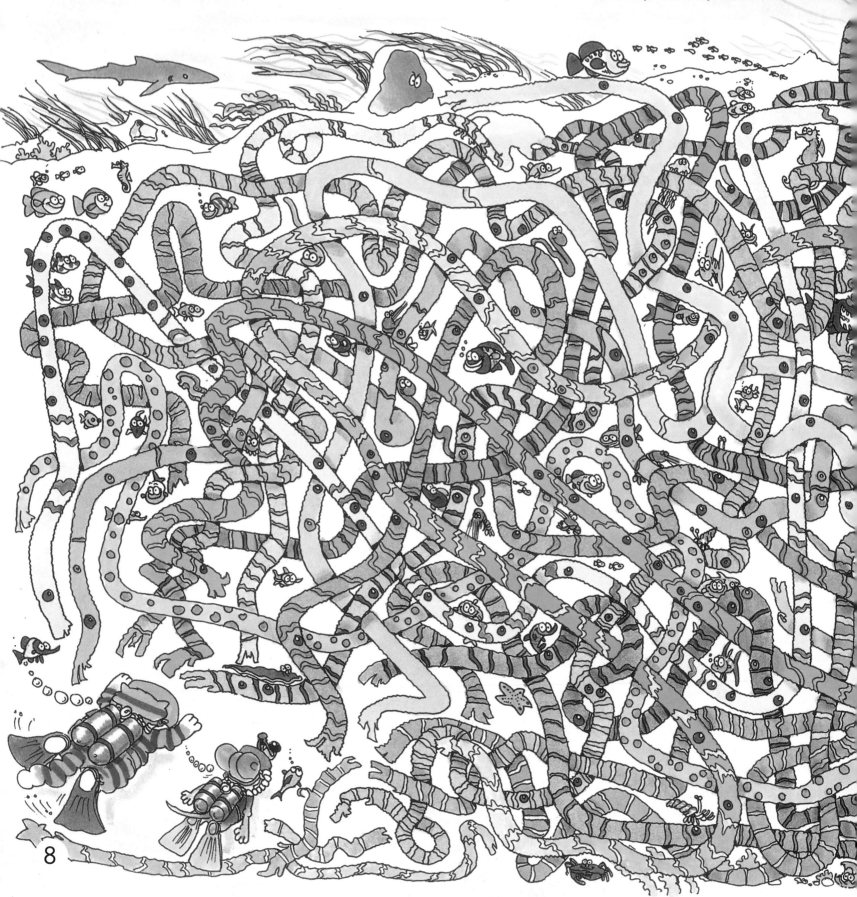

Which way to the wreck?

Queen Conger says that she does know where Penguinland is, but she's not going to tell them because they didn't bring her enough berries. All she will say is that Cat and Mouse should swim to the wreck of the *Angry Kipper* and then go to the surface.

They must swim along underwater pathways to avoid the patrolling sharks that will bite their tails. Also, they must always swim past the seaweed, not through it, because of the poisonous nose-nippers that live in it.

Help Cat and Mouse find their way to the *Angry Kipper* wreck.

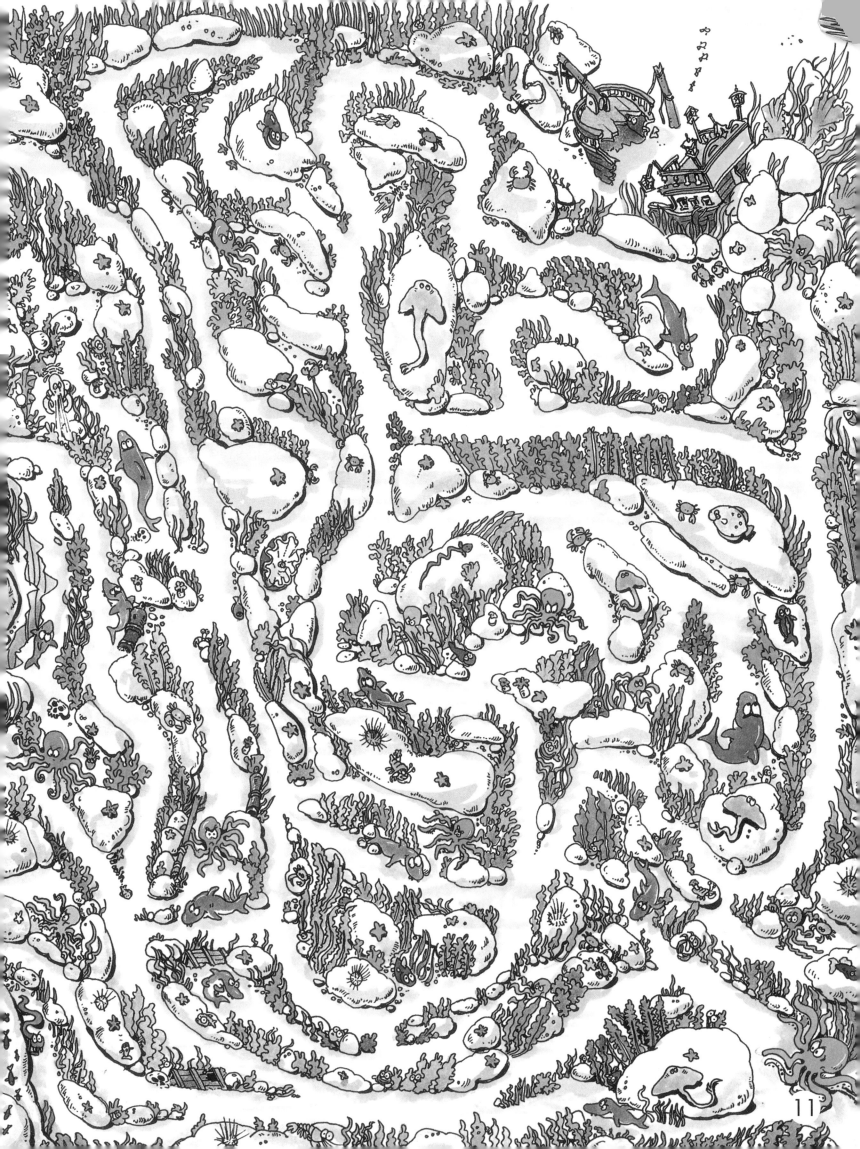

Leaping over the lily pads

As Cat and Mouse rise to the surface, they see a toad sunbathing. They ask about Penguinland and he says, "My Grandpa on the other side of Lily Lagoon will tell you."

Mouse jumps into a lily flower and paddles it through the leaves to Grandpa Toad. Can you see which way he went?

Cat tries to do the same but he is too heavy and his flower sinks. He finds that the dark green lily leaves will stand his weight as long as they have no more than one hole in them. Help him find a pathway across the leaves. He can step over small gaps.

Find Pandora the Parrot

Grandpa Toad is friendly, but can't help Cat and Mouse. He tells them to speak to Pandora the Parrot and points to the tree where she lives. There are lots of parrots in the tree. They ask which one is Pandora. It seems she is sulking in the top branches.

Mouse must climb up carefully, crossing from one branch to another where they touch. The parrots will not move to let him pass by. Pandora is the angry-looking parrot flapping her wings. Which way should Mouse climb to reach her?

Mountain maze

Pandora is pleased to have something exciting to do. "You must go up the mountain," she says. "I will lead you to the mountain steps."

She is too quick for Cat and Mouse, though. Can you help them find their way through the maze of rocks and bushes to the mountain steps?

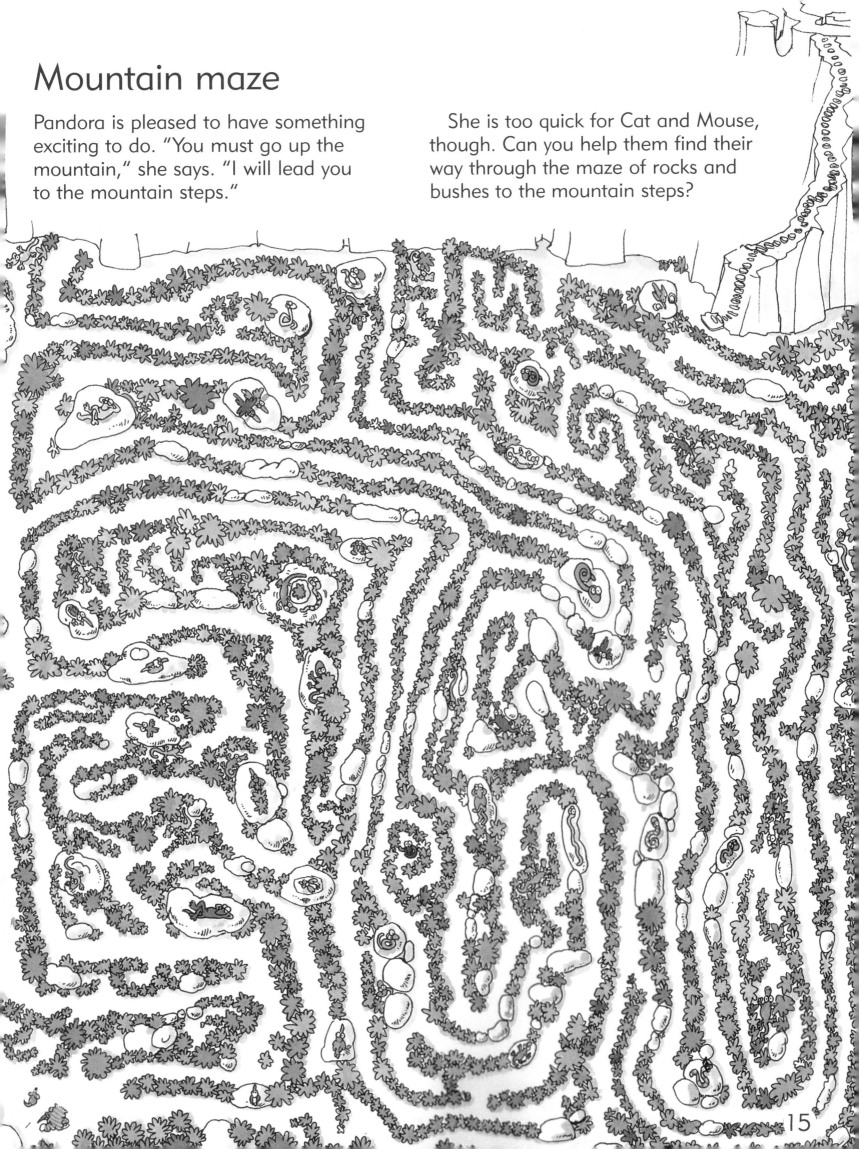

15

Scaling the cliffs to Eagle's nest

Pandora is waiting for them, looking bored. "What took you two so long?" she yawns. "I'm going now. Talk to Eagle. He's over there on the Black Forest Plateau."

Mouse looks at the mountain in despair, but fears they would never find their way back to Lionel's and must go on.

"You must find a route that avoids the nests of flying lizards and dinosaurs. They get very angry if they are disturbed," screeches Pandora as she flies off.

Help Cat and Mouse find a safe route along the treacherous mountain paths.

Follow the flume

Gasping for breath in the thin air, Cat and Mouse find Eagle asleep. They wake him and he tells them that the ice cap they can see in the distance is Penguinland.

"I've made a flume ride down the mountain," he says. "Choose a boat."

Cat looks puzzled. "I can't see any boats."

Eagle points to some logs.

"Oh no," says Cat.

"We'll take number 6," says Mouse.

"How clever of you to choose the deluxe turbo model," says Eagle.

Help Cat and Mouse find their way down to the sea. They must always travel in the direction of the arrows, as these show the way the water flows.

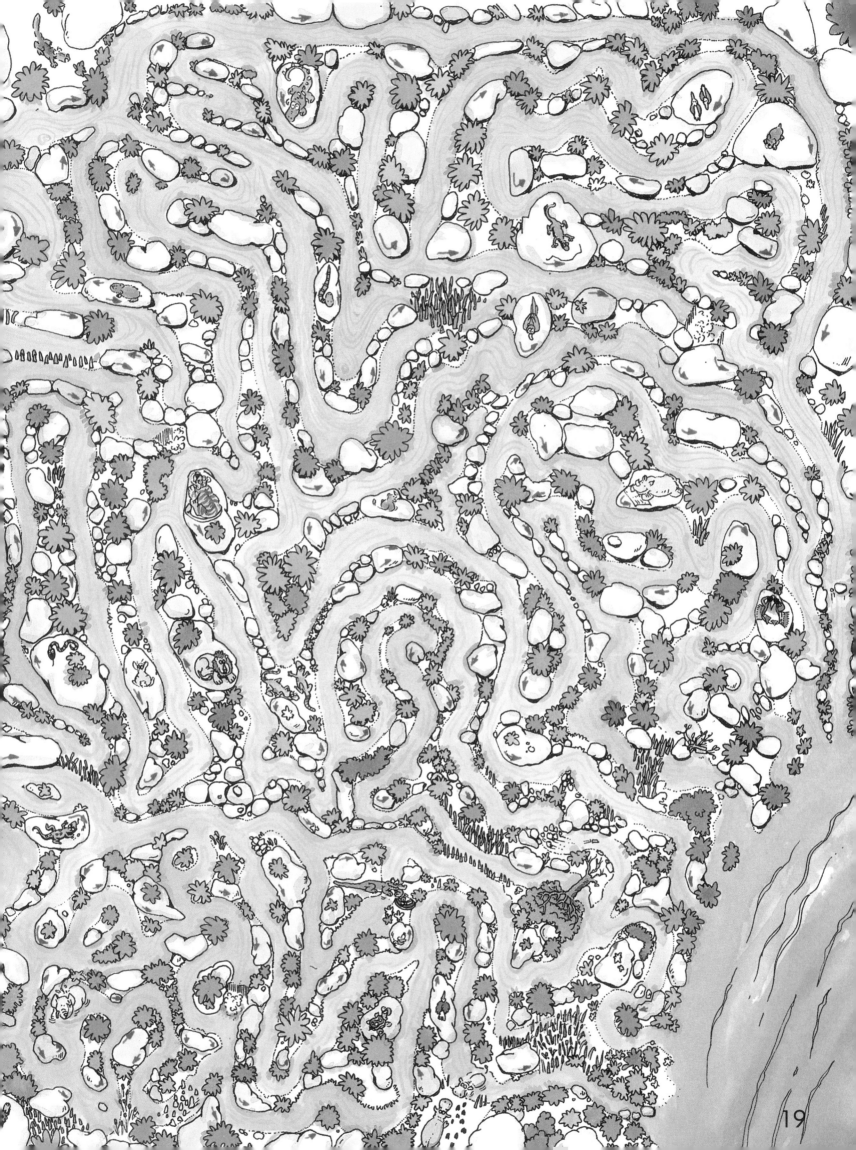

Twisting and turning to Penguinland

"Brrr it's cold down here," says Cat. "Let's find a quick way through all this ice."
They find paddles attached to the side of the log.

"This must be the turbo part," says Mouse.

They paddle towards Penguinland but find they must keep twisting and turning
to avoid the ice. Can you help them find their way through to Penguinland?

20

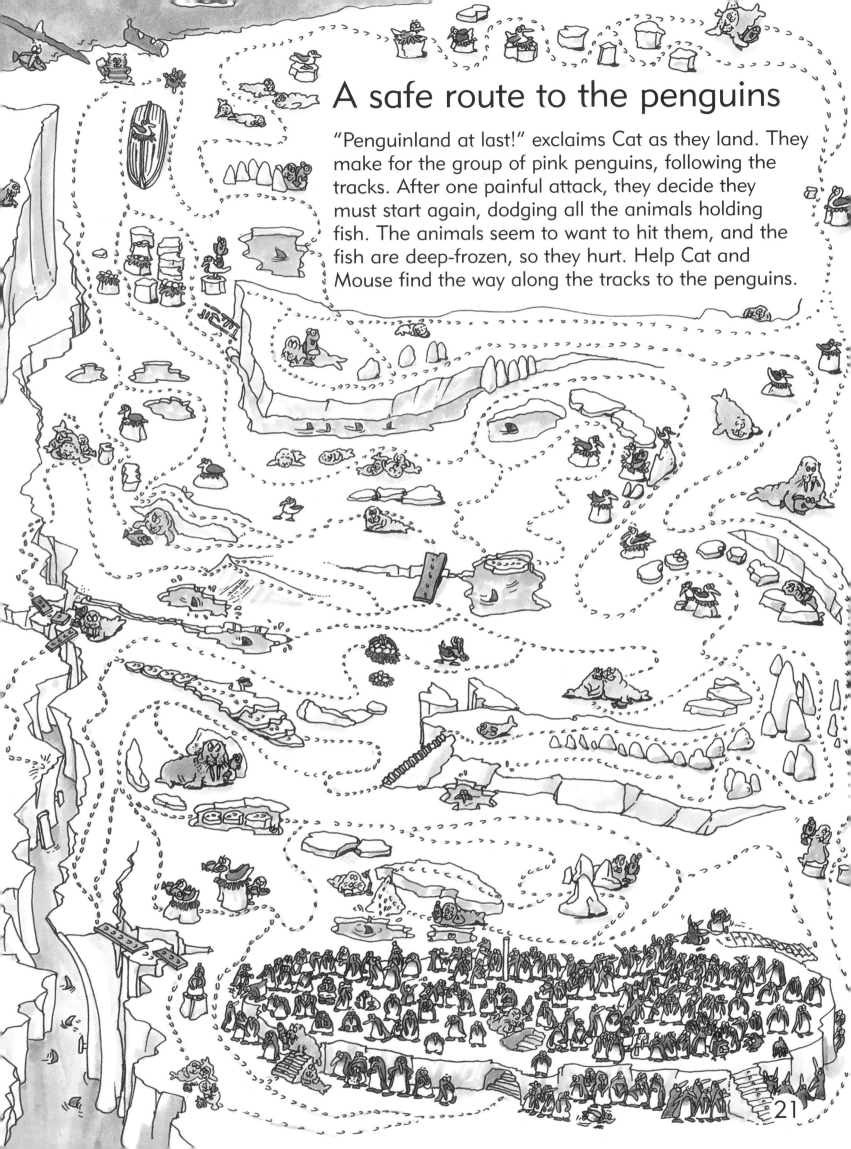

A safe route to the penguins

"Penguinland at last!" exclaims Cat as they land. They make for the group of pink penguins, following the tracks. After one painful attack, they decide they must start again, dodging all the animals holding fish. The animals seem to want to hit them, and the fish are deep-frozen, so they hurt. Help Cat and Mouse find the way along the tracks to the penguins.

Back to the party by plane

"Thank you for bringing Pinkie back to us," says King Penguin. Cat and Mouse look at each other in surprise as they realize that Pinkie has been following them.

"We must get back to Lionel's party," they gasp.

"Oh, that won't take long," says King Penguin. "You didn't come the long way, I hope. We have a daily plane service to Felixham. It's floating in the sea, which is freezing cold, so you'll have to go overland to it," he advises.

Can you help Cat and Mouse find a way to the sea plane? You may have to remind them how to get to Cross Isle from Felixham, too.

Answers

The black lines show the routes through the mazes. Any second route is shown in red.

Pages 2-3

Pages 4-5

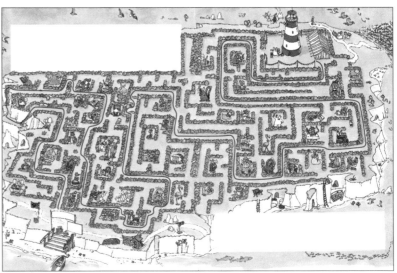

Page 6

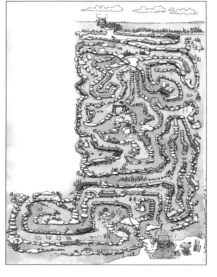

Page 7

Pages 8-9

Pages 10-11

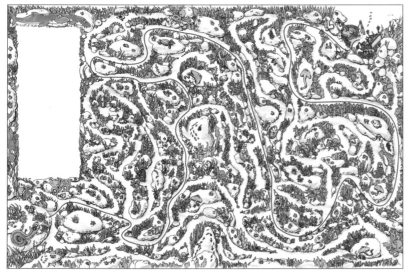

Pages 12-13

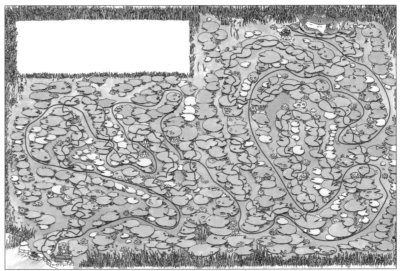

Page 14

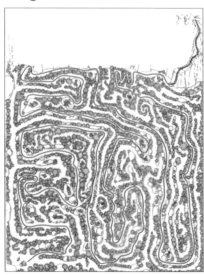

Page 15

Pages 16-17

Pages 18-19

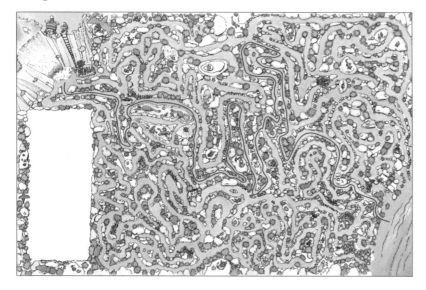

Page 20

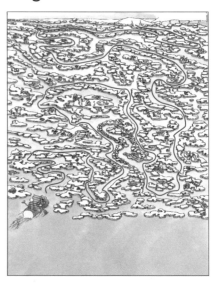

Page 21

Page 22

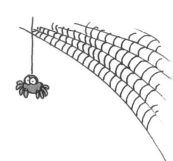

Monster
MAZES

Catching the train

Cat and Mouse have won a Mystery Weekend for Two in a competition. They are looking forward to the interesting food, lively company and surprise entertainment promised in the brochure for the hotel, the famous Adam House.

"I wonder which is our train?" says Mouse. "The lady on the phone said something about spooky and midnight."

"Ah!" shouts Cat, squinting at the departure board. "I know. Follow me. You bring the luggage." Can you find the train Cat and Mouse should catch? Help them find their way to it.

TRAIN	HR
THE GREAT VESTON	11.40
THE RACKET	11.45
SPOOKY EXPRESS	12.00
THE DIPPER	12.30
THE ROYAL SNAIL	12.45
MIDNIGHT EXPRESS	1.00

THE BULLET

CLOCKWORK

SPOOKY EXPRESS

THE GREAT VESTON

MIDNIGHT EXPRESS

THE RACKET

TICKET

27

To the house

After a long journey, the train arrives at the end of the line. There is no one to meet them, but they can see a big house. They set off in its direction and eventually reach an iron gateway.

"Is this the right place?" asks Cat.

Mouse is studying the letters that have fallen off the sign. "A-D-A-M – Adam! Yes, it must be," he says. Cat rushes in, just as Mouse spots a notice. "Beware of the grass," he shouts.

"Yes," shrieks Cat, "beware of the gnomes too – they stab you with their fishing rods."

HOUSE

DO NOT WALK ON THE GRASS IT HAS NOT BEEN FED.

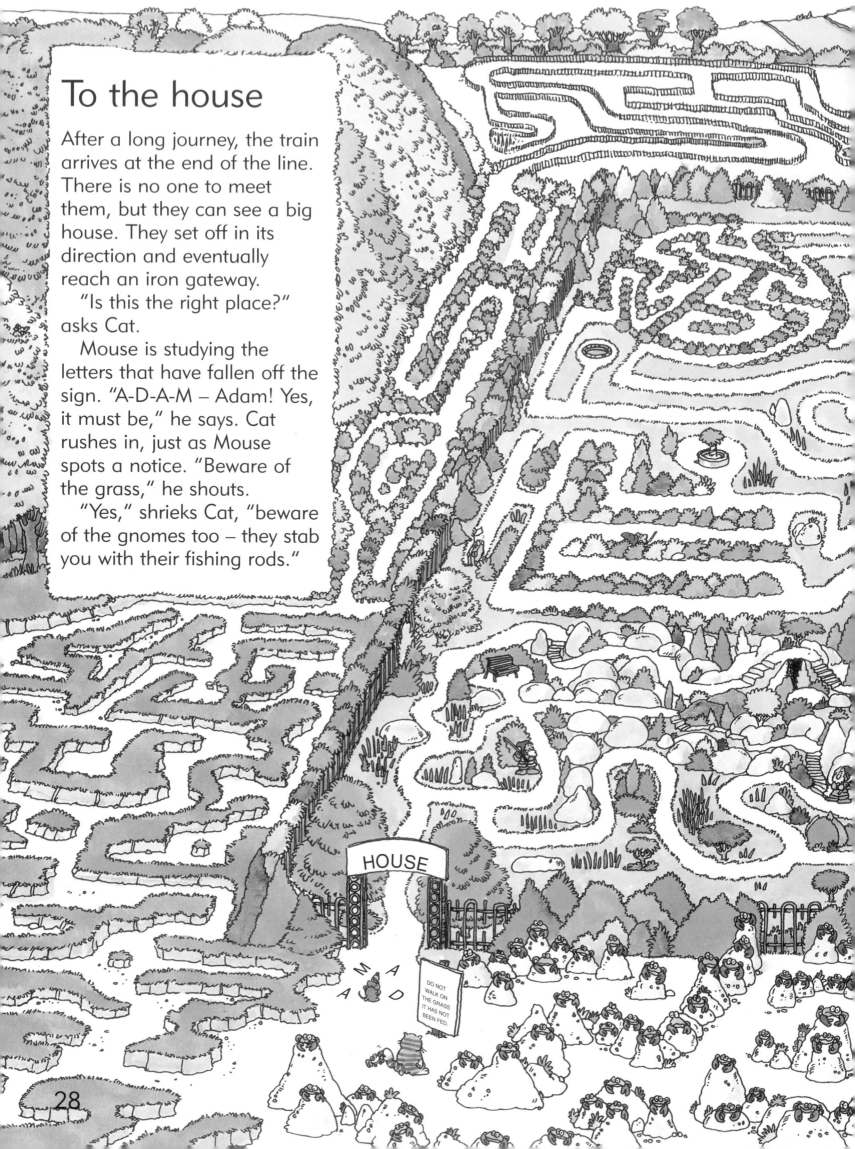

Can you find Cat and Mouse's route from the station to the gateway? Now help them find a way to the house, avoiding grass and gnomes. Cat and Mouse have lost their luggage. There is one bag in every picture from now on. Can you find them all?

DOOR KNOB

The mushroom room

Cat and Mouse reach the house to find all the doors locked. The only way in seems to be through an open window. They climb onto the ledge and peer in. "This room is full of funny mushrooms!" exclaims Cat. He jumps in surprise, knocking a cactus off the ledge, which hits a mushroom and screams as it is engulfed in yellow dust. Help Cat and Mouse find a route to the door that avoids stepping on this type of mushroom.

Danger on the way to the dining room

A toad tells Cat and Mouse to go to the dining room. They haven't gone far when something whizzes over Mouse's head and hits Cat. "Ugh!" says Cat. "Cold rice pudding." It seems the cooks are angry and are hurling yesterday's leftovers at anything that moves. Help Cat and Mouse find a way to the dining room along corridors and through rooms, avoiding the black spots which show where the cooks are.

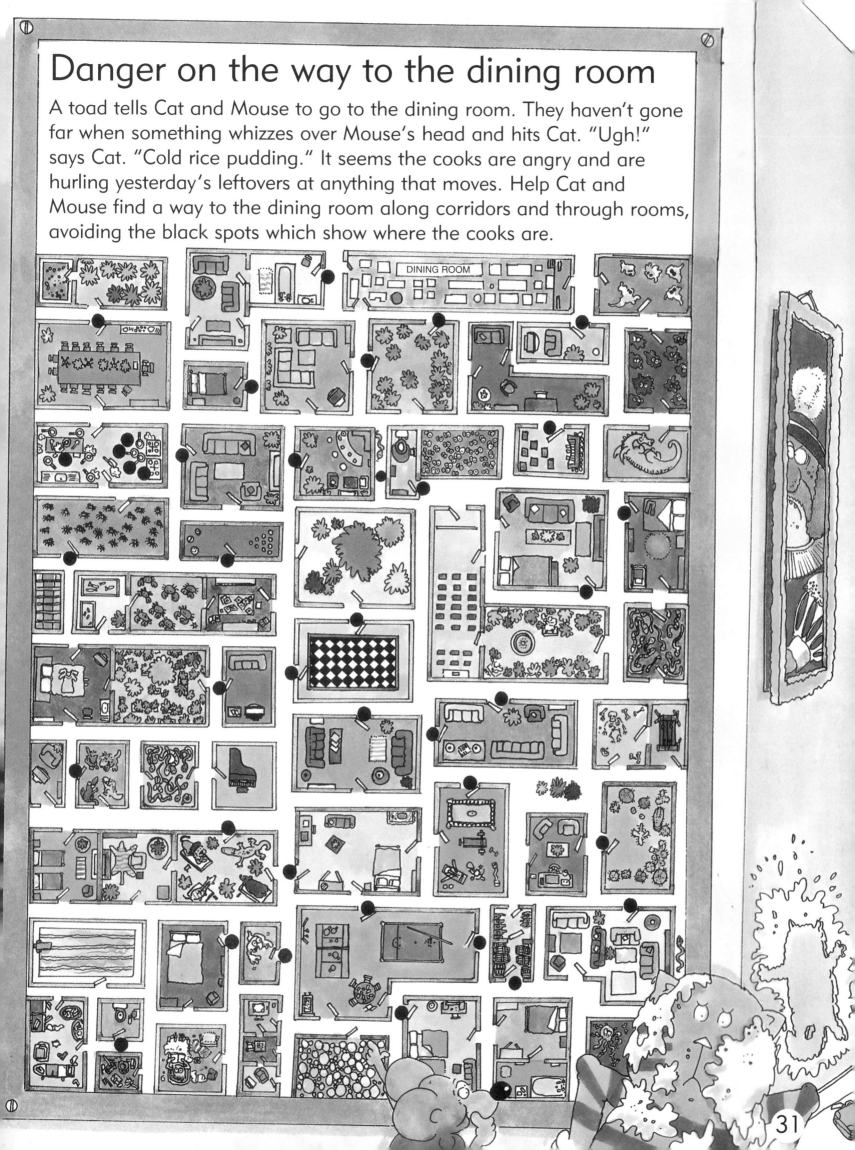

DINING ROOM

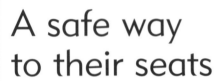

A safe way to their seats

Cat and Mouse are astonished to see that, on reaching the dining room, they find it is full of monsters, who greet them with a great cheer. A red-haired monster beckons to them and points to two empty seats. To reach these, Cat and Mouse must pass a lot of very hungry diners.

They soon find out which ones to avoid: the ones with red forks stab them; the ones with green tongues lick them; and the ones with white fangs bite. Help them find a way to their seats that keeps clear of all these.

"Haven't I seen you before?" says Mouse as they sit down.

"Indeed you have. My name is Elmer. I have been following you all the way."

See if you can spot Elmer from now on. Be careful: he changes shape!

32

A path through the plants

Elmer suggests a tour of the house. Cat and Mouse decide they may as well, as there's nothing to eat. They follow Elmer to a conservatory, where the plants stare at them.

"Where's Elmer?" says Mouse.

"Over there," answers a feelie plant.

"There's something very odd about these plants," says Cat. "We must be careful which way we go."

Help Cat and Mouse find their way to Elmer, without getting too close to the feelies, snappers, stickies and grabbers.

GRABBERS

SNAPPERS

STICKIES

FEELIES

From the statues to the steps

Elmer disappears again – this time into a maze of fog. The clever pair hatch a plan. Cat climbs a statue and spots Elmer. He then guides Mouse to another statue in the middle of the room. Mouse then guides Cat to his statue. They repeat the procedure to reach the steps at the far side of the room.

Can you help Cat find his way through the fog to Mouse and then help both of them reach the steps? Be careful not to pass the monsters that lurk on the way.

Crossing the cellar

Rubbing their eyes, Cat and Mouse find themselves in a cluttered cellar. Hanging from the ceiling is an enormous net which looks as though it might drop down at any minute. It would be impossible to escape from it if it did. Elmer tells them not to worry. It's been there for over 200 years, part of an ancient burglar alarm system. As long as they don't cross any of the red beams, they will be all right.

"There's a party on the roof," shouts Elmer. "You're invited."

Can you find Elmer? Now find a route Cat and Mouse should take to reach him.

Dodging the monsters

Feeling a little tired by now, and wondering how much more surprise entertainment they must enjoy, Cat and Mouse arrive on the roof. A monster party is in full swing. Cat and Mouse look around anxiously for Elmer and at last they spot him. He is waving to them and shouting, "Come and have dinner."

"We should be all right if we go around the backs of the monsters," says Cat. Help Cat and Mouse find their way to Elmer.

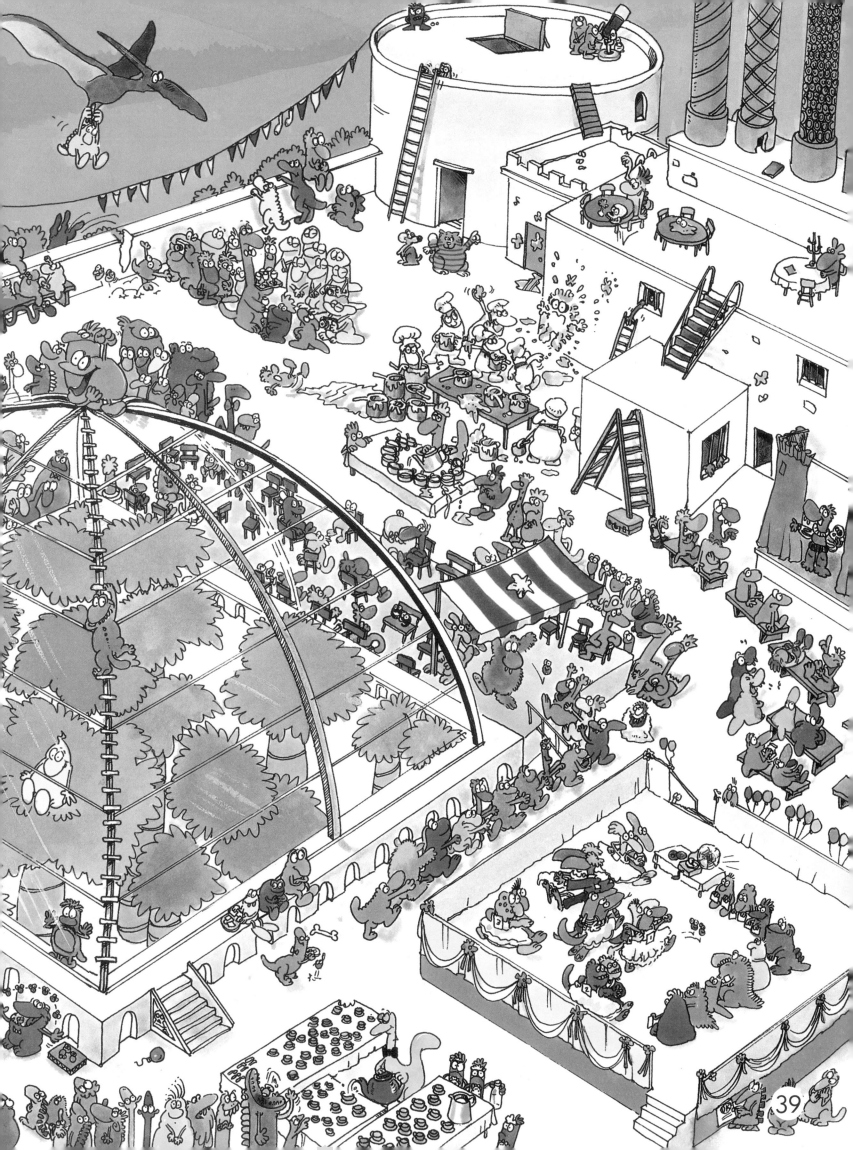

Don't wake the dragons!

After dinner, Cat and Mouse feel better. Elmer introduces them to the monsters, but from a distance, as they will eat anything. He suggests a game of hide-and-seek and disappears. Cat and Mouse don't want to play, but the monsters are creeping closer, armed with knives and forks and bottles of ketchup.

They find Elmer in the doorway of a gloomy room. Elmer darts in. Cat and Mouse creep inside and think they can see lots of snoring dragons.

"I'm going home," says Cat, turning and bumping into the now closed door.

"Don't be silly. This could be fun," says Mouse.

"Psst." Elmer's whisper reaches their ears. "You can walk on the dragons as long as you only step on their red scales. They won't feel that – but be quiet."

Can you find Elmer and show Cat and Mouse which way to go to reach him?

Caught in a cobweb

Mouse trips when he reaches the ledge and he and Elmer fall through a hole in the wall.

"Don't follow us, Cat!" cries Mouse as he hangs from an enormous cobweb.

Elmer shouts that he is all right and tells Cat to find a little door in the dragon kennel. As Cat climbs through the door, he nearly falls into a huge pool of slime. Can you show him a safe way across the room to the pillar at the bottom of the cobweb? He has a piece of plank to help him.

Mouse warns Cat that the red strands of the web are really sticky. He must climb very carefully to avoid waking the giant spider in the corner. Can you show Cat how to rescue Mouse without stepping on a red strand?

Cat and Mouse make a daring escape

As they climb back into the dragon kennel, Cat says wearily, "What now?"

"Let's go home," says Mouse.

They set off through the house, trying to find a way out. There are monsters everywhere, but Cat and Mouse discover they can creep past them. Eventually, they find the front door and run out, much relieved.

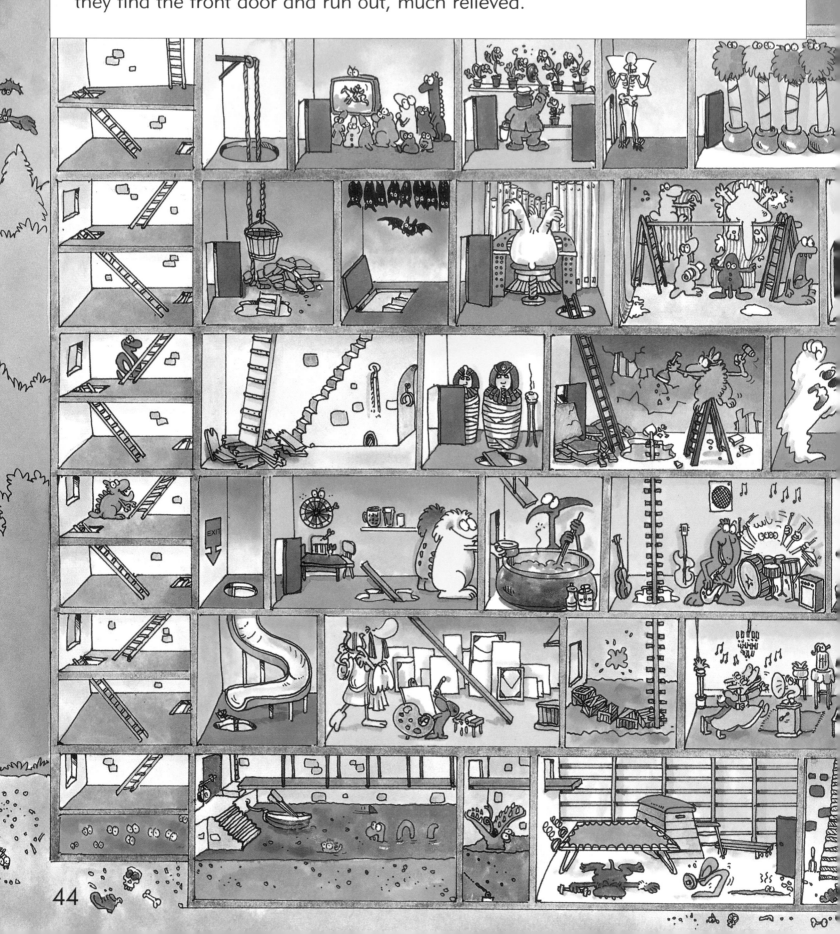

Can you find the dragon room where Cat and Mouse started? Now can you see which way they went to reach the front door?

A dreadful discovery

Once out of the house, Cat and Mouse run like the wind to the railway station, where Mouse checks their tickets for the time of their return train. "Oh dear," he says, "I think we caught the wrong train."

"Never mind," says Cat. "We got here all right, didn't we?"

"Hmm...," says Mouse, looking at labels on some crates, which all say, "A MAD HOUSE".

Cat and Mouse climb the pile of crates and find some newspapers. "Mystery Prize Winners Disappear," they read. "Our correspondent at Adam House in Spoo Quay ponders the fate of the two competition winners who failed to arrive on Friday's Midnight Express." Find a way up the crates to join Cat and Mouse. They made two mistakes about their weekend. What do you think they were?

Answers

The black lines show the routes through the mazes.

Pages 26-27

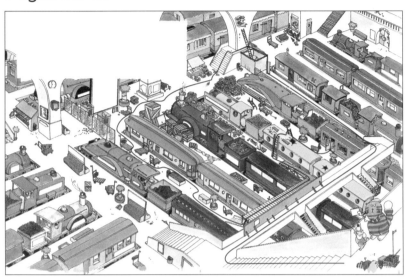

Pages 28-29

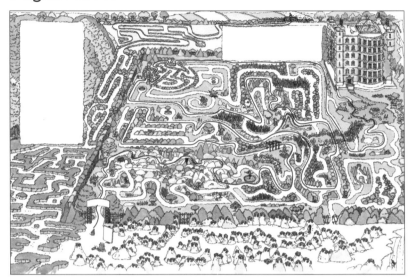

Page 30

Page 31

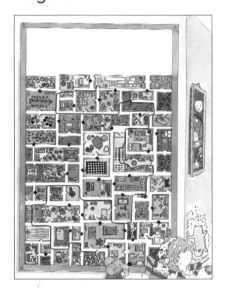

Pages 32-33

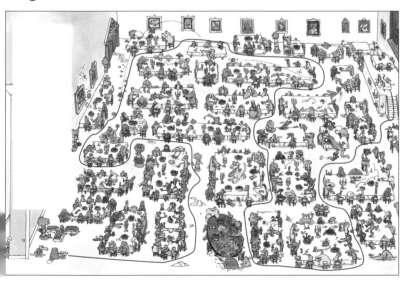

Page 34

Page 35

Pages 36-37

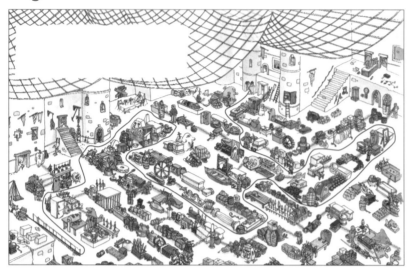

Pages 38-39

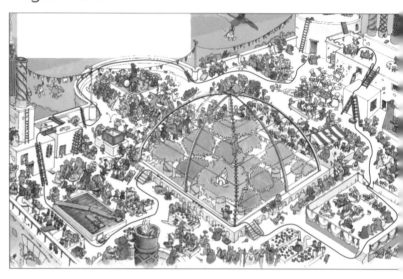

Pages 40-41

Pages 42-43

Pages 44-45

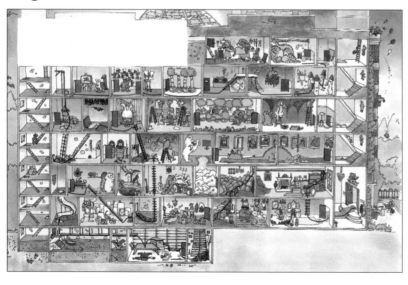

Page 46

Cat and Mouse should have caught the Midnight Express to Spoo Quay, and Mouse arranged the letters to read ADAM when they should have read A MAD.

Treasure MAZES

Across the attic

Cat's Great Aunt Matilda is a world famous explorer and collector. She has just left to go on one of her treasure hunts, leaving Cat and Mouse in charge of her house.

Before she went, she asked them to tidy up for her and baked them one of her very special chocolate cakes as a reward. Cat and Mouse have eaten the cake and are now too full to work. Cat curls up, while Mouse looks lazily around.

Suddenly, Mouse shouts, "Come and look at this!" Cat looks up at Mouse waving a small sack. Cat has to make his way carefully across the attic, as he is so fat and heavy. Can you help him find a way to Mouse? (He can't go anywhere you couldn't.)

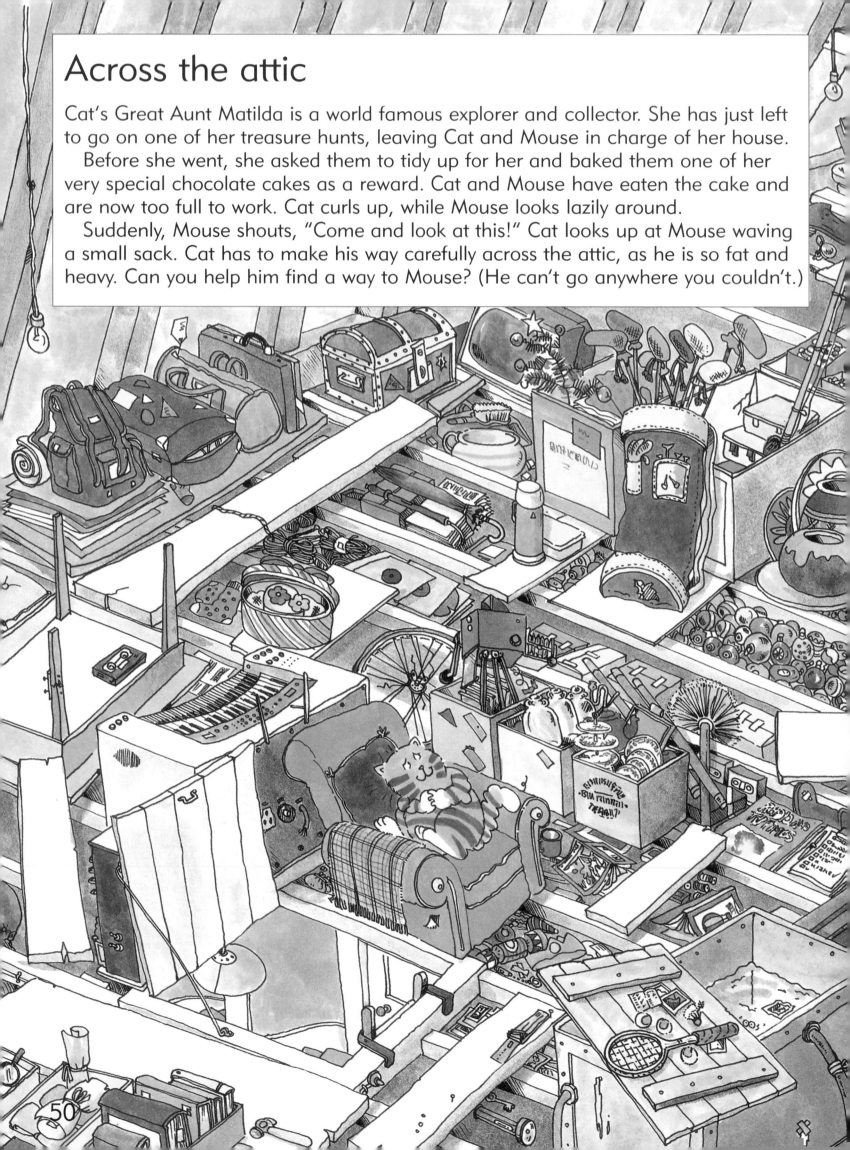

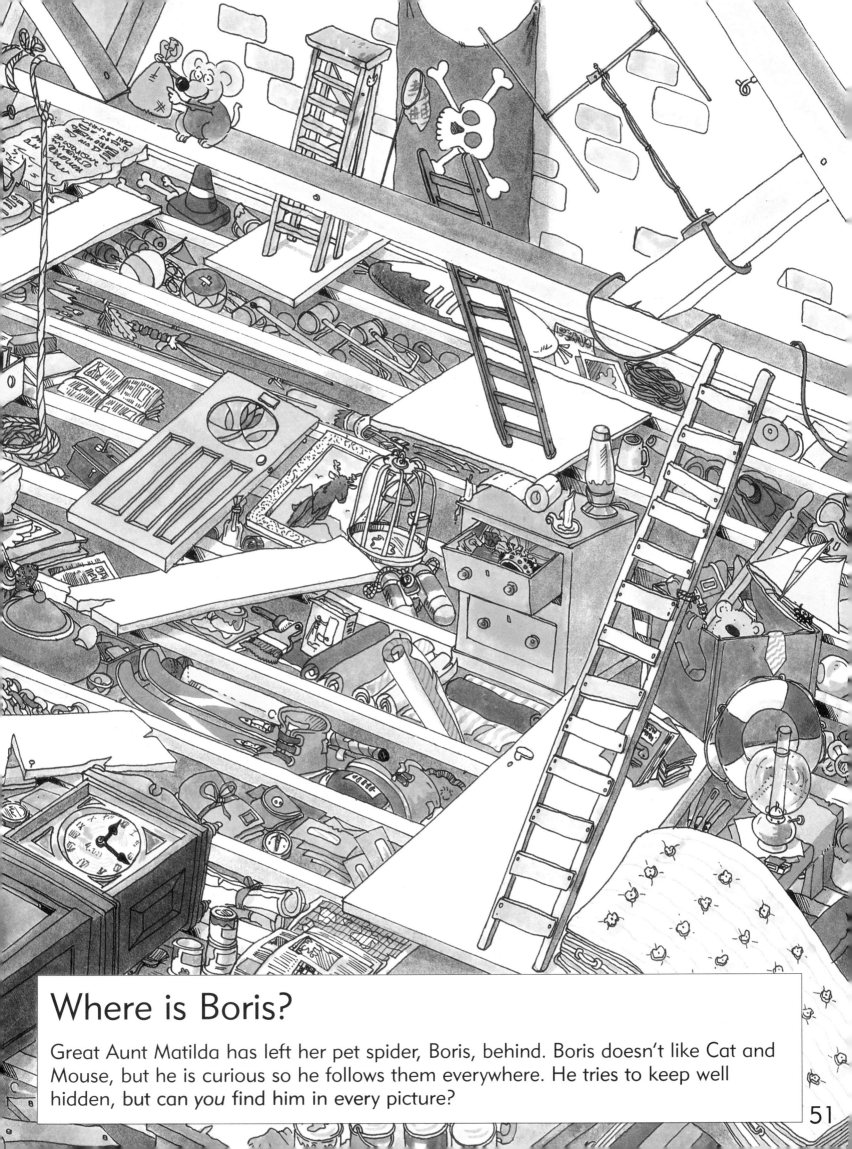

Where is Boris?

Great Aunt Matilda has left her pet spider, Boris, behind. Boris doesn't like Cat and Mouse, but he is curious so he follows them everywhere. He tries to keep well hidden, but can *you* find him in every picture?

The wrong tree

Inside the bag is a map and some superstrong mints. The map shows part of the town. A label on the map says, "Adventure starts at the tallest tree in the park."

Cat rushes to the park but, instead of finding the tallest tree, he goes to the shortest one. Can you find Cat and show him the way back to Mouse?

Now help them both find their way to the tallest tree.

Cat and Mouse are in such a hurry, they don't notice that there is a treasure chest in the park and in all the other places they visit from now on. Can you find them all?

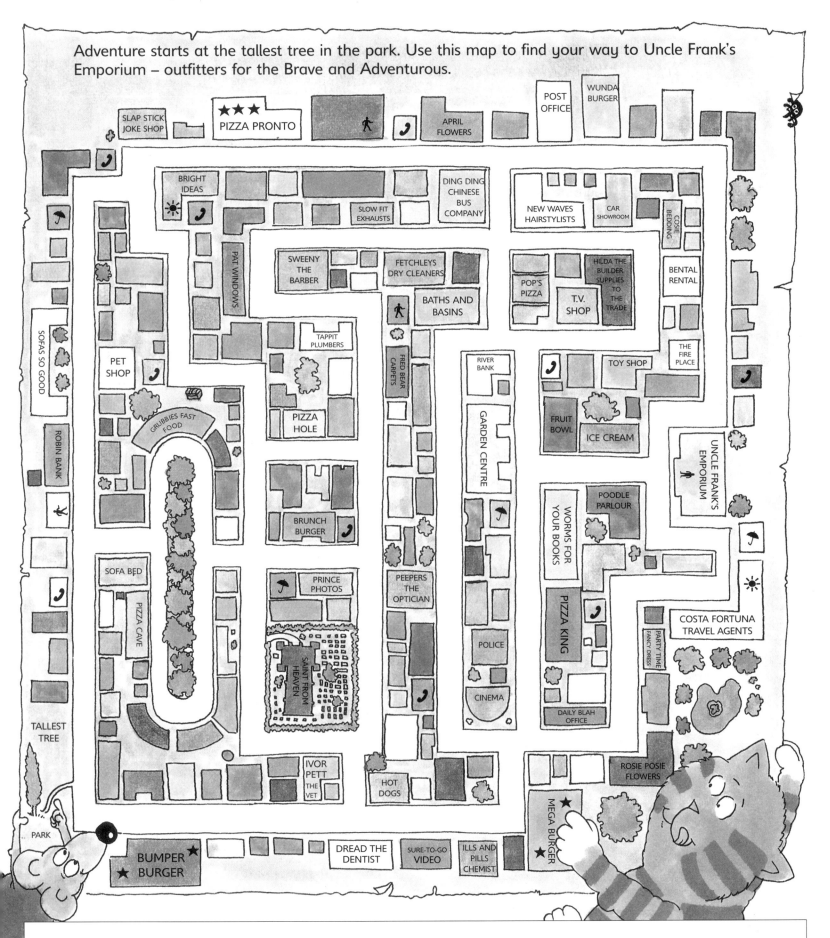

Adventure starts at the tallest tree in the park. Use this map to find your way to Uncle Frank's Emporium – outfitters for the Brave and Adventurous.

Finding Uncle Frank's Emporium

They look at the map again. It tells them to go to Uncle Frank's Emporium, but it is late and they are hungry. Help Cat and Mouse find a route that does NOT pass the front of anywhere they could buy food, or they won't get there before closing time.

A shopping spree

Cat and Mouse rush into Uncle Frank's Emporium. Uncle Frank looks upset. He was looking forward to closing the store and putting his feet up in front of the television.

Mouse offers him the superstrong mints and he cheers up immediately. They are a very special brand which Great Aunt Matilda only brings back with her when she has been up Mount Everest.

Uncle Frank gives Cat and Mouse a shopping list each. He tells them they must collect the items in the order they appear on the list. They must then meet at the nearest mirror.

Can you find Mouse's route through the shop? Now find Cat's route.

white floppy hat
rubber boots
striped sweater
blue T. shirt
snorkel
spade
spotted scarf
telescope
first aid kit
flippers
small backpack
green socks

flashlight
short red walking stick
kettle
plate
cup
bobble hat
sunglasses
large backpack
water bottle
pair of gloves
belt
ball (striped)
umbrella

Where is the rainbow jacket?

Mouse reaches the mirror first. While he waits for Cat, he notices a scrap of paper with some writing on it. It says, "Find the jacket with rainbow stripes and look in the pockets". Help them find the right jacket.

Over the canyon

Mouse finds two very cheap plane tickets in one of the jacket pockets. Cat discovers a golden statue of a camel in the other.

When they arrive at the airport, and find their plane, Cat and Mouse can see why the tickets were so cheap. The plane is extremely old and painfully slow. Worse still, it doesn't actually land at their destination. Cat and Mouse have to parachute to the ground, where they find they have landed on the edge of a very deep canyon.

All Cat and Mouse can see now, in every direction, is desert. After gazing awhile at this vast expanse of sand, they spot a camel and a camel trader some distance away on the other side of the canyon. Help them find their way safely across the canyon to the camel.

(Don't forget to look for Boris and a treasure chest.)

Danger in the desert

The camel trader tells Cat and Mouse that they need to go to the nearest town for their next clue. He swaps his camel for the golden statue.

"Avoid all oases with three trees," he advises. "The dangerous bandits, Los Trioles, often use these as hideouts."

Can you find the route Cat and Mouse should take to get to the town safely? Los Trioles are hiding somewhere in the picture. Can you find them?

Wall walks

As Cat and Mouse approach the town, the camel rears suddenly and throws them to the ground. When they are able to stand up again, the camel has disappeared.

Now they are scanning the town carefully and eventually spot the camel munching his lunch. Cat and Mouse agree that they would get lost down in the streets, so they decide to work their way along the tops of walls, over roofs and up and down stairs.

Can you help them find their way to the camel?

To the coast by helicopter

The camel has a parcel hanging from its neck. Inside it, Mouse finds a model boat, some keys, 20 caramels and a message saying, "Cross the jungle to the coast by helicopter".

After a long, careful search, they find the helicopter. (Look back over the page to see if you can find it, too.)

Cat isn't an expert pilot, and the bumpy flight over the jungle makes Mouse feel ill. Mouse insists Cat land in the first clearing they come to.

Now that Mouse feels a bit better, they take off again, but he can only manage the flight from one clearing to the next without feeling sick.

Unfortunately, some clearings are not safe to land in. Can you help Cat find a route to the coast along a line of safe clearings?

Pay at the pink sign to pass the pirates

Cat lands the helicopter on a cliff overlooking a marina. They wonder if their model matches one of the real boats.

"It does!" mumbles Cat, chewing six caramels at once. They climb down the cliff and realize they are in a pirate-controlled area. A one-legged man gives them a pirate hat, an eye patch and a parrot, and tells them the rules.

At each barrier, they must pay the number of caramels shown on the pink sign. They must have none left when they reach the boat. Which way should they go?

Take a trip to treasure island

Cat and Mouse jump aboard the boat and wonder what to do next. "Ah ha!" exclaims Mouse, looking through his telescope. "There's a signpost on an island over there. I'm sure it says something about treasure on it."

Cat sets sail, but it is more difficult than he thinks to find the way. Can you help him find a safe route to the signpost?

Follow the parrot

As Cat and Mouse stare in the direction of the signpost, their hearts sink. They can just make out the tip of an island surrounded by rings of jagged rocks. Just then, the parrot squawks, "Pretty Polly! Follow me!"

"I hope she knows where she's going," says Mouse. Can you help Polly find a safe way for Cat and Mouse to sail to the island?

The perils of passing the pumpkins

Mouse ties up the boat at a derelict jetty. He and Cat are faced with a steep, rocky slope. There are hazards everywhere, including several rare, but deadly, cat-and-mouse-eating pumpkins.

They feel sure that treasure awaits them in the ruined temple at the top and are determined to find a way up. Can you help them avoid being swallowed by these dangerous vegetables?

Cracking the code

When they eventually reach the temple, Cat spots a carving showing a crown and starts digging around it looking for the promised treasure.

Mouse, meanwhile, is staring at the carving and starts to laugh. "Follow the letters," he chokes. Cat carefully spells out the letters. "After all that," he sighs.

What does the message say? Where should Cat and Mouse go now? Go back and help them find the treasure.

Answers

The black lines show the routes through the mazes. Any second route is shown in red.

Pages 50-51

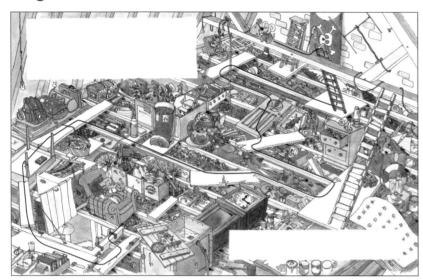

Page 52

Page 53

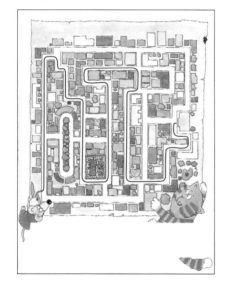

Pages 54-55

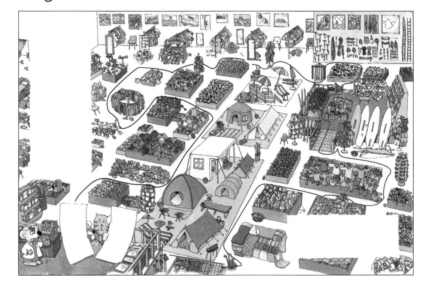

Pages 56-57

Pages 58-59

Pages 60-61

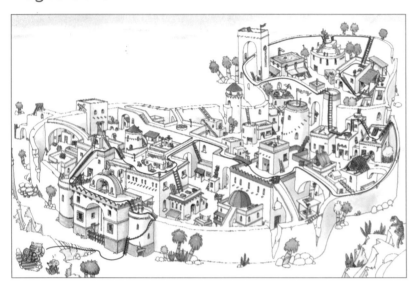

Pages 62-63

Pages 64-65

Pages 66-67

Page 68

Page 69

Page 70

To read this, hold the book up to a mirror. The message reads:

You didn't tidy the attic properly, did you? Look again and you might find this. (Try the top drawer of the chest on page 3.)

This edition first published in 2004 by Usborne Publishing Ltd, Usborne House, 83-85 Saffron Hill, London EC1N 8RT, England. www.usborne.com
Copyright © 2004, 2003, 1992, Usborne Publishing Ltd.
Printed in China. UE. First published in America 2005.